Library
Coaster

Life Cycle of a

Broad Bean

Angela Royston

Heinemann
LIBRARY

First published in Great Britain by Heinemann Library
Halley Court, Jordan Hill, Oxford OX2 8EJ
a division of Reed Educational and Professional Publishing Ltd

Heinemann is a registered trademark of Reed Educational and Professional
Publishing Limited.

Oxford Florence Prague Madrid Athens Melbourne
Auckland Kuala Lumpur Singapore Tokyo Ibadan
Nairobi Kampala Johannesburg Gaborone Portsmouth NH
Chicago Mexico City São Paulo

© Reed Educational and Professional Publishing Ltd 1998
The moral right of the proprietor has been asserted.

All rights reserved. No part of this publication may be reproduced, stored in a
retrieval system, or transmitted in any form or by any means, electronic,
mechanical, photocopying, recording, or otherwise without either the prior written
permission of the Publishers or a licence permitting restricted copying in the United
Kingdom issued by the Copyright Licensing Agency Ltd, 90 Tottenham Court Road,
London W1P 9HE.

Designed by Celia Floyd
Illustrations by Alan Fraser
Printed In Hong Kong by South China Printing Co. (1988) Ltd.

02 01 00 99 98
10 9 8 7 6 5 4 3 2 1

ISBN 0 431 08363 0

British Library Cataloguing in Publication Data

Royston, Angela
    Life cycle of a broad bean
    1.Fava bean - Juvenile literature
    I.Title II.Broad Bean
    583.7'4

Acknowledgements
The Publisher would like to thank the following for permission to reproduce
photographs:
A–Z Botanical Collection Ltd/Moira C Smith p10; Bruce Coleman Ltd/Adrian Davies
p23; Chris Honeywell pp17, 18; Harry Smith Collection pp6, 14, 20, 21, 22, 26/27;
Heather Angel p13; OSF/G A Maclean p19; OSF/G I Bernard pp7, 8, 9; OSF/J A L
Cooke p12; The Garden Picture Library/David Askham p25; The Garden Picture
Library/Mayer Le Scanff p5; The Garden Picture/Michael Howes pp11, 24;
Roger Scruton p4; Trevor Clifford p15.

Cover photograph: Trevor Clifford

Contents

What is a bean?

A bean is a **seed** which grows in a **pod**. We eat many kinds of beans, including black-eyed beans, red kidney beans and broad beans.

I day   I week   2 weeks   6 weeks

These are broad beans. This book shows what happens to a broad bean which is planted in spring.

12 weeks

14 weeks

20 weeks

1–7 days

The bean **seed** is planted in the **soil** with other bean seeds. The soil is watered and the beans begin to grow.

1 day   1 week   2 weeks   6 weeks

root

A **root** grows first. It pushes through the bean seed and grows down into the soil. It grows longer and longer.

12 weeks

14 weeks

20 weeks

2–3 weeks

Now a **shoot** starts to grow. The bent **stem** pushes up through the **soil**. At the end of the stem are tiny leaves.

stem

I day

I week

2 weeks

6 weeks

The shoot has pushed right through the soil. The stem straightens and the leaves begin to open. More **roots** are growing.

roots

12 weeks

14 weeks

20 weeks

3–10 weeks

The leaves open out and turn dark green in the light. The leaves use sunlight, air and water to make food for the plant.

1 day

1 week

2 weeks

6 weeks

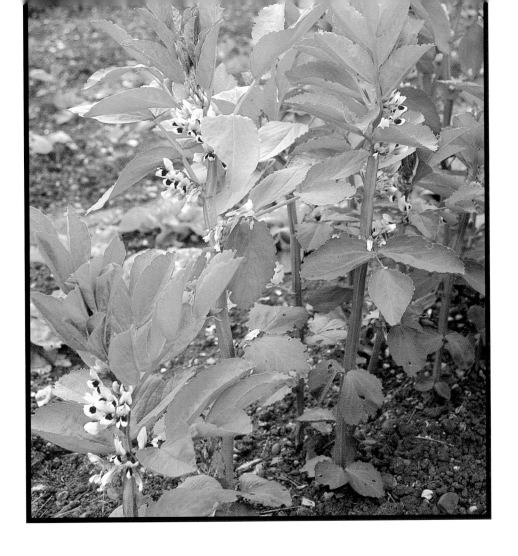

Water from the **soil** passes through the **roots** and up the **stem** to the leaves. The plant grows quickly. Flower-buds begin to form.

12 weeks   14 weeks   20 weeks

11 weeks

A blackfly has laid its eggs under some of the leaves. These blackfly have **hatched** out of the eggs and are eating the leaves.

1 day

1 week

2 weeks

6 weeks

If the plant's leaves become too
damaged, the plant will die.
Ladybirds eat lots of blackfly
and help to save the plant.

12 weeks

14 weeks

20 weeks

12 weeks

Thick **clusters** of flowers open at the bottom of the leaves. The **petals** are black and white.

1 day	1 week	2 weeks	6 weeks

In the centre of each flower are tiny grains of **pollen** and a sweet juice called **nectar**. Insects come to drink the nectar.

12 weeks

14 weeks

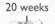
20 weeks

12 weeks

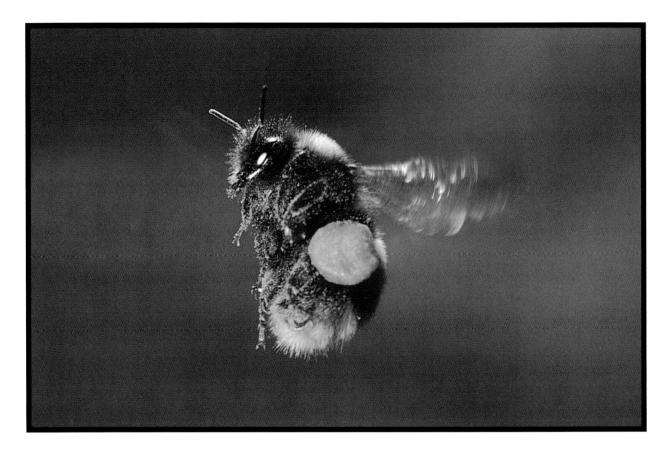

The bee crawls right into the flower. As it sips the **nectar**, grains of **pollen** collect on its hairy legs.

1 day

1 week

2 weeks

6 weeks

At the same time, some of the pollen from another flower rubs off inside this one. This pollen joins a **pod** of **seeds**.

12 weeks

14 weeks

20 weeks

When a **seed** inside the **pod** joins with a grain of **pollen** from another flower, it becomes a new bean. The flower dies and the beans swell.

I day

I week

2 weeks

6 weeks

pods

The beans are protected inside the tough, thick **pod**. As the beans grow, the pod grows longer and heavier.

12 weeks   14 weeks   20 weeks

14 weeks

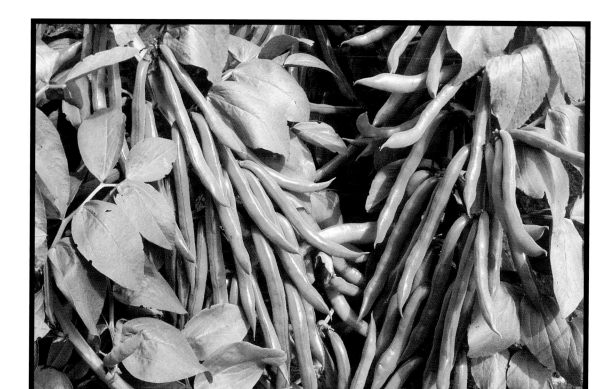

Look how many **pods** are growing on this plant!

1 day   1 week   2 weeks   6 weeks

stalk

The inside of the pod is soft and damp. Each bean is joined to the pod by a short **stalk**. The stalk brings food and water to the bean.

12 weeks

14 weeks

20 weeks

20 weeks

When the beans are fully grown, the **pod** begins to turn black. The plant has done its job and its leaves begin to die.

I day

I week

2 weeks

6 weeks

Some of the pods fall to the ground and split open. Field mice like to eat beans. When a pod splits open they snap them up.

12 weeks   14 weeks   20 weeks

20–24 weeks

Most beans are picked before they are fully grown. They are more juicy to eat then. In autumn the whole plant withers and dies.

| 1 day | 1 week | 2 weeks | 6 weeks |

Not all of the beans are eaten. As they dry, they go hard and brown. These new seeds will be planted next spring to grow into new plants.

12 weeks

14 weeks

20 weeks

A field of beans

Farmers plant beans in huge fields like this one. The **pods** are picked and most are sent to factories to be **frozen** or put in tins.

The plants will be cut up and covered with **soil**. As the plants rot, they slowly break up and become part of the soil.

Life cycle

1 day

1 week

2 weeks

6 weeks

12 weeks

14 weeks

20 weeks

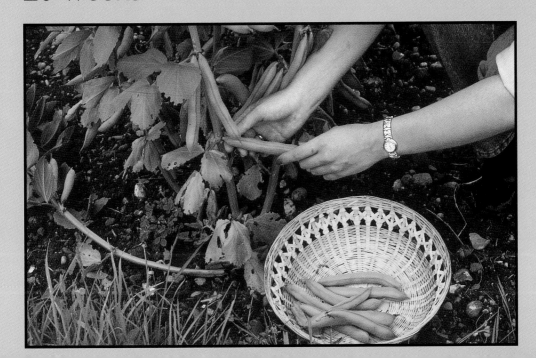

29

Fact file

In just four months a broad bean grows from a seed to a plant as tall as an adult person.

The bean that Jack planted in *Jack and the Beanstalk* was a broad bean.

One broad bean plant can produce over 300 beans.

In Ancient Greece and Rome, rich people would not eat broad beans because they thought they would damage their sight.

Glossary

hatch   to be born out of an egg

nectar   a sweet, sugary juice in the centre of a flower

pod   a tough, thick shell that surrounds the beans

pollen   fine yellow dust made in the centre of a flower

root   part of a plant under the ground which takes in water from the soil

seed   the fruit of a plant which can grow into a new plant

shoot   the first stem and leaves of a new plant

stem   the stalk that supports the leaves, flowers and fruit of a plant

Index